COVER LETTER E-NOTES
THE MODERN WAY TO LAND INTERVIEWS

LISA RANGEL

CONTENTS

Introduction	v
1. Cover Letter e-Note — What's That?	1
2. Do You Need a Cover Letter E-Note?	3
3. 10 Mistakes to Avoid When Writing Your Cover Letter e-Note	5
4. 8 New and Time-Tested Tips to Write Powerful Cover Letter e-Notes	12
5. The Simple Cover Letter e-Note Structure	18
6. 14 Types of Effective Cover Letter e-Notes	23
Next Steps	43
Also by Lisa Rangel	45
About the Author	47

COPYRIGHT © 2023 Chameleon Resumes LLC

This document is intended for private, individual use only by the individual purchasing the document. Transmission, distribution, duplication or public use by any means (electronic, mechanical, recording, photocopying or otherwise) is prohibited without express written consent from Chameleon Resumes.

ISBN: 978-1-7333176-3-4

DISCLAIMER: While the author has used her best efforts in preparing and producing this ebook, she makes no guarantees, representations or warranties with the respect to the accuracy or completeness of the contents of this book and specifically disclaim any implied warranties for sale for fitness for a particular purpose. No warranty may be created or extended through affiliate or marketing partnerships in print or online sales and marketing materials. The advice and strategies contained herein are the opinions and based off client experiences of the author and may not be suitable for your situation. You should consult with a proper professional where appropriate. The author shall not be liable for any loss of profit, income or commercial damages, including but not limited to special, incidental, consequential or any other damage.

INTRODUCTION

Cover letter e-notes are magical, concise correspondences that move job-landing efforts forward faster in today's electronic world.

Gone are the days of long, attention-draining letters received in the office snail mail. With so many people working from home post-pandemic, how would you even send mail to the office to be received in a timely manner? And as for manifesto-type emails making detailed points as a substitution for conversation — they're also antiquated.

No more.

Short and to-the-point e-notes are the way to go, and they're here to stay. I say, "Thank God!" because no-one has time to read lengthy cover letters whose only actual job is to ask, "Can we have a chat?" Because ultimately, setting up a meeting should be the clear purpose of every e-note and related follow-up message.

So in this ebook, I'll share the simple ideas behind the construction of an effective cover letter e-note — and plenty of samples for you to dig into. It's tricky to know how to write an effective note, and being inspired by e-notes that are proven to work is a good place to start writing your own cover letter e-notes. Kudos to you for starting here!

The sample e-notes you'll find in this book are short but powerful. These e-notes have worked for me and my clients; your experience may vary.

Remember — Nike conveyed magic in its three word tagline "Just Do It." Effective cover letter e-notes will need a few more words than that to be effective, but short and sweet is the goal of this new communication category.

Let's start by getting clear on what a cover letter e-note really is.

CHAPTER 1
COVER LETTER E-NOTE — WHAT'S THAT?

These days, a cover letter e-note sits in the body of an email to which your resume and any other additional relevant information is attached.

Hence the name: cover letter e-note. It's a cover letter, sent electronically. And it's short, like a note.

Don't attach an e-note document separately in an email or embed it into the resume document. Place it into the body of the email with any accompanying information to supplement the cover letter e-note.

It's not just a post-pandemic practice, either; we started putting cover letter e-notes in the email body instead of a physical letter before the pandemic for a few reasons:

- Emails are faster than snail mail.
- Emails with attached electronic resumes can get the resume uploaded to an applicant-tracking system

faster than scanning a physical resume document. Recruiters prefer electronic resumes and the "note" that is the body of the email is now where the cover letter e-note goes.
- We used physical cover letters before the pandemic to get noticed, for a non-urgent opening or an exploratory chat. Since no-one sends mail anymore, a physical letter had a higher chance of getting noticed. But post-pandemic, with so many people working from home, physical mail may not get to the recipient in a timely manner, if at all. So e-notes are now best.

We can easily convert a traditional cover letter into a cover letter e-note. If you have a traditionally formatted cover letter, take the body of the letter and use that content as the basis of your cover letter e-note. It's that easy.

CHAPTER 2
DO YOU NEED A COVER LETTER E-NOTE?

The purpose of a cover letter e-note depends on whom you are talking to: some say it's to introduce you to a prospective employer or connection to land a meeting (a chat or interview). Others say the purpose of an e-note is to complement your resume or bio to further tell your story — but keep in mind, your resume will carry most of the weight to landing the coveted interview for you. And then there are still others who say a cover letter e-note is pointless since no-one reads them anymore.

I say they're all correct. Studies are inconclusive about whether e-notes truly matter. The bottom line is, some hiring managers swear by them and others ignore them.

Which is why you always need to have a good cover letter e-note ready to go: you never know who's going to receive your resume.

A cover letter e-note, like a resume, LinkedIn Profile or executive bio, is a tool that can help you land an interview.

On its own, a cover letter e-note is not a magic elixir that will land an interview for you every time. And not having one won't kill your chances of landing an interview if you submitted your resume to a recruiter who never reads e-notes. (I was a recruiter who didn't read e-notes.)

But a poorly written cover letter e-note CAN kill your chances of landing an interview. And if an e-note is required and you don't have one, it could stop your application dead in its tracks.

If you submit your resume to a recruiter who devours cover letter e-notes like my husband devours greasy bacon cheeseburgers, and you don't have a solid e-note coupled with your resume, your candidacy may be as done as that burger.

You see my point... you may need a cover letter e-note or you may not. The important thing is to be ready with a good one that will bring about action from your reader when you need it most.

That's the point of this ebook: to help you write a cover letter that will give you the best chance of landing that interview.

CHAPTER 3

10 MISTAKES TO AVOID WHEN WRITING YOUR COVER LETTER E-NOTE

Before I get into the different types of cover letter e-note and how to write them, I want to set the stage by sharing the ten most common mistakes I see job hunters make. I want you to avoid them, and write the most effective cover letter e-note for you.

Making any of these errors can put your resume and cover letter e-note into the "delete" bin. So be sure to keep these tips in mind when you apply the lessons in this book:

Cover letter e-note mistake #1:
Copying other cover letter e-notes verbatim

Now, I know you just bought a cover letter e-note book that contains samples so you can learn how to write cover letter e-notes. And now I'm telling you not to copy the samples in here.

You may think, "Hang on — that's not fair!"

Well, think about it. Once it's in a book and many people have access to it, it's only a matter of time before a recruiter will see a parade of similar-sounding cover letter e-notes across their desktop monitor.

Job seekers often copy e-notes and unknowingly apply for the same job. Guess what happens then? The recruiter finds multiple applicants with similar sounding e-notes. Coincidence? Nope. Both candidates copied from the same book.

The key is to use what you read here (and anywhere else) as inspiration to help you write your own variation.

Write from your heart. This is one sure way to be original and stand out: nobody has the exact experience and personality that you do.

Cover letter e-note mistake #2:
Writing a poor subject line

Modern day cover letter e-notes don't go into the physical mailbox anymore. They arrive as e-notes now. And in crowded inboxes, e-notes need an attention-grabbing subject line to inspire the reader to want to read it.

Put yourself in the recruiter's shoes: they work on an average of 30 to 40 open job requisitions at once, according to the Society for Human Resource Management's (SHRM's) HR Knowledge Center. They receive hundreds of resumes every week.

A subject line that helps the reader understand your intention and helps sort out where your application goes can make a huge difference.

Cover letter e-note mistake #3:
Making the e-note all about you

Writing from your heart is great — but be sure that's not all you write about. The common mistake here is to focus too much on yourself and not enough on helping the recruiter / hiring manager connect the dots as to why they should take up your invitation for an exploratory chat and / or how you're qualified for the role. If you interrupt someone's day — as all emails do — don't talk only about yourself. Incentivize the reader to want to connect with you with a well-written, interesting, relevant letter.

Cover letter e-note mistake #4:
Forgetting about your audience

If you make the mistake of talking only about yourself, you are making another mistake in failing to factor in what your audience wants to read. Remember: the purpose of the e-note is to get the reader interested in speaking with you further. So, as you write, remember to throw in enticing information that will make the reader want to continue the conversation. If you tell them everything in the e-note, they may decide then and there they don't want to have a chat.

Make it interesting, make it relevant, and make them want to know more about you.

Cover letter e-note mistake #5:
Forgetting the tl;dr rule (too long; didn't read)

If your cover letter e-note is too long, people won't read it. Most e-notes — almost all of them — should be no longer than a page. Around 100-200 words maximum for most e-notes is just fine. You don't want to tell your life story or write a manifesto starting from your high school graduation.

Remember, the purpose of the e-note is to help you to book a conversation then actually have the conversation. You don't want to put so much information in the e-note that it's holding up your side of the conversation and. If it does that, the reader doesn't need to contact you—you already told them everything they think they need to know.

Cover letter e-note mistake #6:
Using your cover letter e-note for therapy

The cover letter e-note is a marketing tool — not a place for cathartic confessions. Generally, you should avoid bringing negative things to light in your e-note. You can address diplomatically in your interview such issues as:

* Why are you leaving / have you left your last job?
* Why you were fired
* How your boss didn't see your potential
* Exiting a toxic environment

This is a "first impression" communication and none of these thorny issues need explanations now. The interview is a much better place for this, but you won't be able to have that conversation if your cover letter e-note puts them off meeting you altogether.

Cover letter e-note mistake #7:
Sounding like everyone else

When I was a recruiter in NYC, I worked on placements for some pretty high-profile companies in fashion, finance, and media. And if I had a dollar for every cover letter e-note that included, "I would LOVE to work for X organization," or, "I have always been a fan and I would be so honored to work at X," I would be rich.

Fan-girling or fan-boying all over a prospective employer doesn't set you apart from the thousands of applicants that apply. In fact, it makes you sound like everyone else.

Frankly, wanting to work there because it's a great company should be a given, right? So don't sound like everyone else and, instead, write something unique about yourself that shows you did your homework.

Cover letter e-note mistake #8:
Making typos

This error goes without saying, but I'm saying it anyway. Avoid typos. Here's the thing about typos: some people are now more forgiving about typos considering how fast business moves combined with the 24/7 nature of how many industries run. But many people don't forgive typos — and you don't know who those people are.

So put yourself in the best position possible by avoiding them altogether.

Read your cover letter e-note aloud to yourself before you send it. This tactic is one of the best ways to discover grammar errors and misspellings. Reading the document aloud can help you find typos the spellchecker missed.

Cover letter e-note mistake #9:
Restating your resume in prose form

The cover letter e-note should not be a regurgitation of your resume in long-form writing.

Use the e-note as an opportunity to connect your background with a unique situation at the company you're applying to, or a personal connection with the reader based on your research.

Repeating your entire resume in paragraph form will not win anyone over.

Cover letter e-note mistake #10:
Making your resume dependent on your cover letter e-note

I know this is a cover letter e-note ebook, but I would be remiss if I didn't mention the mistake many people make with their cover letter e-note regarding their resume. The resume should be able to stand alone and be independent of the e-note. The resume should not need the e-note to make sense of the resume, since resumes and cover letter e-notes get separated all the time — and, as mentioned earlier, not every person reads e-notes.

Making your e-note tell the story of your resume is a risky move. Don't do it.

These are the most common mistakes I see people make with their cover letter e-notes. In a nutshell: be yourself, write a note that's interesting to the reader, relevant, and helps you stand out.

CHAPTER 4
8 NEW AND TIME-TESTED TIPS TO WRITE POWERFUL COVER LETTER E-NOTES

New *and* time-tested? Yes, I have blended new and timeless advice here in this chapter, and when you combine these eight tips together, your cover letter e-note will be super effective.

1. MAKE YOUR COVER LETTER E-NOTE DIFFERENT FROM EVERYONE ELSE'S

Meaning: don't copy sample letters verbatim. Use them to inspire you to craft your own, as that's how you truly come across as unique.

Telling a potential employer you problem-solve uniquely, then using a canned letter that could be sent to anyone by anyone over and over, without any customization or evidence that you did any research, contradicts your claim of having unique problem-solving skills.

Similarly, don't copy and paste the same newly-written cover letter e-note to every person to whom you reach out — even if you wrote it yourself. Recruiters and hiring managers can sense a mass cut-and-paste job a mile away.

Do some research and customization to make sure your e-note is crafted specifically for each recipient.

2. WRITE FROM THE READER'S PERSPECTIVE —NOT JUST YOURS

Before you write your cover letter e-note to a prospective employer or network connection, consider who's going to read it. Put yourself in their shoes. Imagine them at their desk, trying to balance work and home life, having demands made upon them, and knee-deep in their humanity. Feel it? Great.

Then, with that image in your mind, frame what you are about to say to that person and consider how you want to connect with them.

The key point here is to come from a place of meeting them where they are versus coming from a place of "here is everything about me" when they didn't even ask.

3. PIQUE THE READER'S INTEREST AND TELL THEM HOW YOU FOUND THEM

Lead with how you came to email them and how you found their name, because that's usually the first question recipients have: "How did you get my name?"

People want to know the source of your communication

effort to determine if they should reply or ignore. (This is blunt, but it's true.)

Phrases like, "We have some mutual connections in common," or, "We share the same alma mater," or, "William Jones encouraged me to reach out to you," can have one of two effects:

1. The reader is genuinely interested and will double check the mutual connections, or will check your background since you share the same college, or they love William Jones, so anyone William refers will be interesting to them.
2. They aren't genuinely interested… but they may look up the common connections before deciding to blow you off. Or they won't care that you went to the same college, but since it's a good school, they'll check out your background before deciding to ignore you. Or they really don't like William, soooo they just won't reply.

Regardless, the goal will have been achieved in five out of six instances—they checked out your background. Which is all you really want—a chance to be evaluated and seen. Nothing happens without that evaluation, so this is the goal of piquing the reader's interest.

4. INCORPORATE YOUR RESEARCH WHENEVER POSSIBLE AND RELEVANT

Using research in a cover letter e-note never goes out of fashion. You might want to refer to an article or a trending social media thread about the company, or perhaps use public research about the recipient (in an appropriate, non-stalky, fan-like manner, of course). Weaving in research can help you to customize your letter, stay relevant, and sound different from everyone else.

5. DON'T BE AFRAID TO MENTION ONE AWESOME FACT OR PERSONALITY TRAIT ABOUT YOURSELF THAT IS PERTINENT

Don't be afraid to follow up with something interesting about yourself. After you pique their interest, if appropriate, this is a chance to "Wow" the reader.

Share a relevant win or personality trait that may reinforce why they might want to talk with you briefly. Maybe you solved a similar problem they have that's publicly known. Or maybe you see an opportunity to do what you have successfully done somewhere else. Or maybe you share an experience working for a similar high-profile company, which is a badge of honor in your circles. This isn't bragging; it's highlighting your points of interest.

6. BE SPECIFIC AND CONNECT THE DOTS FOR YOUR READER

Whether it's an exploratory chat or applying to a specific job, help the reader out by being specific in your brief e-note. Don't expect them to know what you want or why you're emailing them. They most likely won't know. So be clear and specific to increase your chances of success with your e-note.

7. KEEP IT SHORT

Do not write a prose version of your resume as your cover letter e-note. It will earn a big yawn from the recruiter. Keep your e-note short and to the point for the greatest chance of success. People just don't have the time, the interest, or the attention spans to read long, unsolicited emails anymore. So cut to the chase and more people will read what you send.

8. END WITH A CLEAR CALL TO ACTION. HUMANELY...

At the end of your e-note, ask for that chat appointment you want. Don't be afraid to ask.

Share your contact info. Offer your calendar link (I'll explain this in the next paragraph) and let them know you're open to times that work for them. I suggest offering both options and not choosing just one.

Some people will love it if you send your calendar link; others will hate it. If you include both options, you allow your recipient to decide what's easiest for them, without imposing unwanted work on them. This shows that you understand there are many ways to conduct business, and you're willing to be accommodating.

When I say "use your calendar link," I'm suggesting that you sign up for an electronic calendar function such as Calendly, Acuity, TimeTrade, or vcita. There are other companies beyond these and I'm not endorsing any one company. They're all good, and which one will be best for you depends on your needs and work habits.

Using an electronic calendar can reduce the back-n-forth email tennis that can often happen while we try to set a meeting time. And it prevents the awkwardness of holding times offered that haven't been confirmed.

You'll see how I use the calendar function in some of the e-note samples later in this ebook.

Lastly, when I say "humanely," I mean you should state flat out that you expect nothing from this e-note. People don't want to be taken from — they want to give.

When I send cover e-notes, I include something like, "no obligation or pressure" or "no agenda" — then if they take me up on a meeting, I'm not asking for anything right away — or at all. I go into the meeting intending to find out how I can help them.

The age-old networking mantra "give to get" holds true when job-seeking, too. There's another old saying from Zig Ziglar: you will get all that you want in life if you help enough other people get what they want.

CHAPTER 5
THE SIMPLE COVER LETTER E-NOTE STRUCTURE

It can be difficult to know where to start with a cover letter e-note, but there's a simple and effective structure you can follow to give you the best chance of success. A successful cover letter e-note has five parts:

1. The e-note subject line
2. The salutation
3. The body and length of your e-note
4. The call to action
5. The signature

When all parts of the cover letter e-note are include, coupled with engaging content, you increase your chances of landing interviews and meetings.

I suggest applying persuasive copywriting principles alongside the recruiting insights I am sharing with you here.

Write your cover letter e-note to capture the attention of the reader. Competing priorities often distract recruiters from the notes they receive. As a former recruiter for 13 years, I can tell you from personal experience this is true. Because of those distractions, plus the volume of applications, and their limited time, recruiters look for clues that they should continue reading as they skim your letter. They typically don't truly read it—they scan it, subliminally looking for evidence that you're the right person for this role. So write your cover letter in such a way that you keep their interest and attention in 10-15 second increments.

Motivate the reader to keep reading using this 5-part cover letter e-note format.

1. E-NOTE SUBJECT LINES

Subject lines of cover letter e-notes are extremely important and job seekers now need to pay attention to them when crafting an outreach e-note for their job search.

Recruiters work on many job openings at any given time, so it can be hard to keep track of applications and messages. Subject lines that give the recruiter all the information they need at a glance will be extremely helpful to them — and start you off on a good foot. If you write your subject line so that it shows what job you're seeking, plus shares a little about you, you'll often get the best traction. Recruiters need help sorting through the influx of resumes they receive — so showing the position you are applying for is very helpful to an inundated recruiter.

An effective attention-grabbing tactic is the copywriting technique of sticking to only eight words in the e-note subject line. If you look at any email in your mobile device inbox, you often won't see past the eighth word in the subject line. So you increase the chance of your e-note being read if we can read all the words of the subject line.

Include the role of the job you are targeting plus one of the following to make your subject line unique to you: your name, a result you have accomplished, something memorable about you, a piece of info to show you did your research, a mutual connection or work interest.

2. SALUTATION

Address your cover letter e-note to an individual person. Always take the extra time to research a prospective boss, designated hiring manager, or networking connection about the job you want.

Never address your cover letter e-note "To Whom It May Concern" or some other impersonal recipient. That shows a lack of effort. Always find a name to use in your greeting as it will always be appreciated.

3. BODY AND LENGTH

Here is your one chance to be interesting — your first impression. It doesn't have to be grand. Focus on the simple.

Think as you write: "What would make them want to check out my profile and reply?"

Cite relevant achievements in your background that will interest the prospective employer. Connect these to how you came to be interested in this role. This is your opportunity to share something unique and relevant about your history that could pique the interest of the reader, and make them want to learn more about you through an interview.

The length of a cover letter e-note shouldn't be more than a scroll or two on a phone or a screenshot on a desktop. For many e-notes, 100-200 words at most is suitable.

There are always exceptions to every rule, but do revisit the 10 Mistakes to Avoid When Writing Your e-Note chapter, so you don't break the "too long; didn't read" rule and turn your e-note into a treatise.

Generally, paragraphs should be one or two sentences — maybe three — and not dense. There should be plenty of white space around each paragraph to make it easy to read.

4. CALL TO ACTION

In copywriting terms, a call to action asks the reader to take action — it does what it says on the tin. With your cover letter e-note, your call to action will be to request a formal interview, casual conversation, or exploratory meeting. Tell the reader how they can reach you and give them options for your availability. Make it easy for them to reply and book that meeting.

Your closing tone should be "humane." Review #8 under 8 New and Time-Tested Tips. Using an electronic calendar management tool can help make meeting arrangements easier.

5. SIGNATURE

Your electronic signature should include your name, phone number (if not in the body of the e-note), email address (for convenience), and any social media profile links (such as a LinkedIn URL). You may or may not attach a resume or bio, depending on the nature of your cover letter e-note request (informal meeting or formal interview).

CHAPTER 6
14 TYPES OF EFFECTIVE COVER LETTER E-NOTES

Whether you're networking proactively or purposefully job seeking, you will require a cover letter e-note. Choosing the appropriate letter type as inspiration for your cover letter e-note can set you on the right path to getting a reply. Here are different cover letter e-notes for the varied circumstances you'll encounter as you search for a new job and/or maintain your career network.

CORPORATE ALUMNI CONNECTION COVER LETTER E-NOTE

You don't have to know someone personally from college to reach out to them. I believe that when you or your parents paid for tuition, that payment included access to the entire college alumni network. If you are 15 to 30 years out of school, reach out to alumni younger than you. If you are 5 to 10 years out of school, reach out to people older than you. Don't just reach out to your age bracket.

You can use this e-note type for high school alumni, sorority/fraternity groups, art groups, sports teams, and many groups from educational pursuits.

Here is a sample e-note to show you how you can do that:

SUBJECT LINE: Fellow Cornell grad reaching out

Dear Matt,

I'm reaching out in the spirit of networking as I see we both graduated from Cornell (you in 1998 and me in 2006). We bring different graduating class perspectives to the table. I also really enjoyed that piece you wrote in ____. Congrats!

I was hoping you might be able to chat for 15-20 minutes so we can learn more about each other's work since college. No agenda or obligation.

If you can carve out some time, here is my calendar link, or feel free to shoot over some times that work for you, and let me know your preference for meeting (phone, Zoom, etc.). I'm happy to accommodate.

Thanks for reading this far,
Madeline
Phone/email/LinkedIn URL

CORPORATE ALUMNI CONNECTION COVER LETTER E-NOTE

Writing to corporate alumni is not very different from writing to college alumni. Look for people on LinkedIn and other sources who used to work for the same company you did and use that as a point of leverage to connect.

You don't have to know them personally. They may still be at the company and you no longer work there — or vice versa. Or maybe neither of you work there anymore, which can be a point to bond over. It's the shared experience that someone may respond to.

Here is an example of how to use this information for an exploratory interview:

SUBJECT LINE: Piedmont Alum interested in your career path

Dear Idira,

I am reaching out in the spirit of networking, as I see we both used to work at Piedmont Partners. I'm intrigued by how you made a pivot from the finance industry to the consumer healthcare industry. Well done! Would you be open to having a 15-20 minute chat about your experience, as I'm looking to do something similar?

No obligation, agenda, or solicitation for a job, I promise :) I am interested in learning how you did it, as that may give me some ideas on how to accomplish this myself.

And, of course, if there's any way I can help you, I would be honored to do so.

If you can carve out some time, here is my calendar link, or feel free to shoot over some times that work for you, and let me know your preference for meeting (phone, Zoom, etc.). I'm happy to accommodate.

Thank you for considering my request. Look forward to your thoughts when you're able to share.

Ben

Phone/email/LinkedIn URL

COLD APPROACH COVER LETTER E-NOTE

Many job seekers are finding success because they're expanding their networks and reaching out to people outside their first and second-degree circles.

To make this happen, sometimes you need to reach out to people you don't know, which can feel awkward. Try some of these approaches.

The following e-note works particularly well in Twitter Direct Messages or less mainstream business contexts, but it can be successful in many instances.

It will have a lower response rate than a letter leveraging a connection or a shared experience, but it's still a tool to keep in the job search toolbox to expand your next step.

There are two versions of this e-note for you to try here.

Version 1:

SUBJECT LINE: Your marketing campaign made me sign up!

Dear Sharon,

I found your marketing campaign for the _____ speaker series inspiring! The approach was refreshingly human and powerfully simple. I am looking forward to attending.

Would you be open to having a 15-20 minute exploratory conversation in the spirit of networking? No agenda and no pressure. I am a mid-level marketer (link to my profile if it helps: <<insert LinkedIn URL>>) who loves to connect with forward-thinking leaders in the industry to simply chat and see where it leads.

If so, here is a link to my calendar, or feel free to send me any times that work for you.

Many thanks!

Sam

Phone/email/LinkedIn URL

Version 2:

SUBJECT LINE: Human Resources Leader requesting to chat

Dear James,

I'm reaching out to explore Human Resources leadership roles within the _____ organization after being inspired by _____.

The accomplishments I bring (here is my LinkedIn profile outlining my specific relevant wins <<link>>) attracting top talent and leading them to surpass corporate goals during this pandemic time could be of value to your area.

Would you be interested in scheduling an exploratory meeting to determine if what I do can help _____ achieve its upcoming goals?

I realize I'm reaching out in an unsolicited manner, so thank you for reading my request. If this is an avenue you would like to explore, let me know what time options are best for you, or here is a link to my calendar, if this is more helpful to you.

Thank you for your time and attention.

I look forward to hearing from you when the time is right.

Sincerely,

Monica

Phone/email/LinkedIn URL

CONFERENCE ATTENDEE COVER LETTER E-NOTE

Attending conferences virtually or in person can be a super easy way to expand your network.

Most people are attending for human interaction, so it's important to take advantage of this reason for attending the conference.

This is a sample letter to use with anyone you saw attending the conference, perhaps because they used a hashtag on Twitter, or maybe you saw them in a Zoom offshoot room.

Most people will appreciate a tasteful, simple request to chat casually.

SUBJECT LINE: Chat with a fellow TechZine Conference attendee?

Hello Raj,

Hope this note finds you well. I was recently in a Zoom room with you at the TechZine conference. I found your comment on ____ helpful and was wondering if you'd be open to a phone chat to further explore what you described? No agenda or pressure. Just looking to connect in the spirit of networking.

If it's easy for you, here is a link to my calendar to schedule a chat. Or send me a couple of times that work for you and I'll accommodate your schedule as best as I can. Looking forward to chatting when you can.

Be well,

Mark

Phone/email/LinkedIn URL

SPEAKER CONNECTION COVER LETTER E-NOTE

This letter has worked for me and my clients for years because speakers like to spread their message.

Speakers are also typically connectors. So having chats can often lead to further conversations with others in each of your expanding networks.

Here is an example that has repeatedly worked:

SUBJECT LINE: Interest in your presentation at MarketingPro 4.0

Dear Sonya,

I was enlightened by your ___ presentation at the recent MarketingPro 4.0 conference. I hadn't thought of approaching B2B clients in that way before and I'm excited to test this in my own work at ___ as a ___. I'll keep you posted!

Would you be open to a 15-20 minute chat to explore opportunities between us? I have no agenda or expectations, but I found your work intriguing and I would like to learn more about how you work with clients. Additionally, I can expand on what we're doing here at ___. We can simply have an exploratory chat and see where it takes us.

Thoughts?

If it's easy for you, here is a link to my calendar to schedule a chat. Or send me a couple of times that work for you and I'll accommodate your schedule as best as I can. Looking forward to chatting when you can.

Be well,
Chris Mitchell
Phone/email/LinkedIn URL

RESEARCH-INFUSED COVER LETTER E-NOTE

Weaving in research from trade or industry publications to reach thought leaders is a wonderful way to make inroads into new connection sources.

It's also a way to make a communication effort unique to the reader. Typically, the more customized and unique your communication, the more likely you are to get a reply.

SUBJECT LINE: Your article ____: something I learned and put to use

Dear Dr Jones,

I recently discovered your article titled "____." Thank you for writing it and sharing your research. I applied what I learned from you in a recent conversation with a colleague and it made all the difference in the outcome. I wanted to share this success story with you. So thank you.

Would you be interested in having a 10-15 minute chat, as I am conducting a job search in the ___ field. I had a couple of questions and would be very grateful to gain your insight as to how I could approach the ___ organization, on which you seem to have some knowledge, as I saw in your bio and prior research. I'm not asking for referrals, as you're unfamiliar with my work. I am seeking advice on my approach, if you can offer some, once I share my thoughts. No pressure or obligation, of course, as I imagine your time is in demand.

Please advise me if you have the availability to chat and, if so, when might be the best time to do so.

Thank you for considering my request. I appreciate your attention and what I have learned from you so far.

Many thanks,
Marian Richards
Phone/email/LinkedIn URL

SOCIAL MEDIA REFERENCE COVER LETTER E-NOTE

I am a big fan of taking social media offline and making social media... well, social! This e-note works wonders for networking and lite-vibe exploratory chats.

SUBJECT LINE: Would you be open to chatting offline?

Hello Mike,

I follow you on Twitter and have been reading your posts for a while (here is my profile: <<Twitter link>>). I always find what you post fun and intriguing.

I, too, have a background in ___, and thought it would be fun to connect offline. Would you be interested in having a chat in the spirit of networking? I have no agenda and there is certainly no obligation. I'm simply looking to make social media "social" and have a chat.

Thoughts? If you're open to chatting, feel free to use my calendar link (here) or simply reply to this email with a couple of times that work for you.

Jack Banthan
Phone/email/LinkedIn URL

GENERAL NETWORKING CHAT / VIRTUAL COFFEE MEETING E-NOTE

This e-note can be an inspiration for reaching out to people cold "in the spirit of networking" — which is my favorite phrase for all things networking and trying to meet new people.

Here's an example of an e-note that has produced a reply in past scenarios:

SUBJECT LINE: Our mutual interest in X

Dear Marilyn,

Your answer to Mark William's recent social media post about ___ caught my attention, and I felt compelled to reach out. I thought your point was spot on! Would you be open to having a phone chat (or Zoom, whatever you prefer) in the spirit of networking?

What you've written and shared is interesting and I was thinking we could have a non-committal chat and see where it goes (like networking at a live conference, but you know... it's Covid, so let's Zoom chat LOL).

No pressure or anything. Let me know if you'd like to connect offline using my calendar link (here) or shooting over to me a couple of times that work for you to chat. I'll do my best to accommodate you.

Many thanks,
Ashlee Wathins
Phone/email/LinkedIn URL

REFERRAL COVER LETTER E-NOTE

If a bonafide person has referred you into an organization, that's really helpful and you should use it. It's best to be direct and humble with this type of e-note.

SUBJECT LINE: Referred by Melanie Rodriguez

Hello Ang,

I hope this email finds you well. My name is Lina Mulligan. Melanie Rodriguez encouraged me to reach out to you as someone who might be able to offer insight on my endeavors to apply to ____ for the ____ position.

Melanie shared that you've always been helpful with clear, realistic advice on how to position her experience for certain roles, and credits your advice with helping her throughout her career. She encouraged me to connect with you to find out if you had 10-15 minutes to chat to possibly offer similar insight to me.

Would you be open to a brief chat? I completely understand if you cannot do so, as I know your time is in demand. However, if you can connect, I would be grateful. Let me know how to proceed to accommodate your schedule.

Many thanks,
Lina
Phone/email/LinkedIn URL

LEVERAGE MUTUAL CONNECTION TO CHAT COVER LETTER E-NOTE

You don't have to be referred to use a name, if you share a common connection. You can simply tell them that the fact you have a mutual connection inspired you to reach out. There's always a risk, as the recipient may not know the mutual social media connection or may not even like them. But it's a tactic to use strategically when you think the risk to do so is low.

SUBJECT LINE: Reaching out because we have INSERT NAME in common

Dear Leia,

We share a mutual connection in ____ on LinkedIn and I wanted to reach out in the spirit of networking to introduce myself.

I am a ____ who could possibly add value to the ___ initiatives in your organization, based on ____. Would you be interested in a 15-20 minute exploratory chat to see if we have any synergies? Here is a link to my calendar or feel free to share time options that work best for you and I'll do my best to accommodate. Thank you for the consideration.

Much gratitude,

Muhammad El-Shafi

Phone/email/LinkedIn URL

EXPLORATORY INTERVIEW COVER LETTER E-NOTE

While many of the letters included in this guide focus on landing casual networking chats that can easily lead to genuine job leads, they aren't always direct requests for an interview. The Exploratory Interview e-Note is a direct request e-note and includes a bit more background about you to incentivize the reader to want to connect with you.

Here's an example that has worked:

SUBJECT LINE: Jason Lee suggested we connect

Hello Jane,

A mutual acquaintance, Jason Lee, gave me your name as a contact for an informational interview. I read your recent article on mobile marketing for healthcare providers on LinkedIn. I thought your app ideas were interesting and would welcome the opportunity to chat further.

My background is in strategic business marketing and consumer communications. I'm interested in exploring positions in marketing strategy and technology in the healthcare industry and implemented a somewhat similar marketing effort last year. From research and in speaking with Jason, I feel that speaking with you may provide a mutual benefit.

Would you have time to chat with me? I appreciate any time you might have. If it helps make it happen, you can find my schedule here, or let me know any times you're available and I will do my best to accommodate.

Thanks and best regards,
Chioma Langford
Phone/email/LinkedIn URL

TARGETED JOB COVER LETTER E-NOTE

E-notes that target specific job openings are most effective when they connect the dots for the reader between what the job requires and what you bring to the table. With most e-notes, it's best to keep them very brief, but this one could be a little longer.

Use the target job description to craft the target job cover letter e-note and to decide which candidate achievements to include in your text.

Here's an example of what's worked in the past for job seekers:

SUBJECT LINE: Marketing Director — Melody Maren — increases leads/revenues

Dear Ms. Johnson,

I am interested in the Marketing Director position listed on the CMO.com association website. Designing and executing online marketing campaigns successfully in the consumer products industry is where my expertise lies, and positions me to add value immediately to the role. I've attached my resume for your reference.

In 2020, I assembled a team of four to accomplish the following achievements for the XXX brand product line:

- Increased lead generation by 11% and generated 6% more in sales ($270,000) compared to 2019, with an 8% lower marketing budget.
- Drove lead generation, which came from improved Google ads and integrated Facebook/Instagram marketing using an influencer marketing content strategy that contributed to the lead increase.

- In a separate marketing campaign, developed relationships with 19 high social media profile brand influencers to promote XXX products that were tracked to add $1,340,000 more in sales in 2020.

Prior to 2020, I have a pattern of measurable success in the areas required by the position description as well as a strong interest in the mission of ___. The pending sale of my organization has inspired me to express interest in your open position.

I welcome the opportunity to have a discussion on how I could contribute to the organization's short and long-term goals.

Sincerely,
Melody Maren
Phone/email/LinkedIn URL

THIRD-PARTY RECRUITER / EXECUTIVE SEARCH COVER LETTER E-NOTE

Third-party recruiters work for companies that pay them to find talent. They don't exist to find jobs for candidates. If you have a background that means the recruiter's paying client wants to hire you, the illusion is that they are finding you a job. But make no mistake, the recruiter is not doing that. They are simply delivering a product to their paying client — that product being you.

When contacting a third party recruiter / executive search consultant, acknowledge that during the conversation they will evaluate you to determine if you're suitable for their client. If the recruiter thinks that presenting you to their client will make them look good, believe me, they will want to chat.

And if they think you understand how recruiting works and may have referrals to other quality, placeable candidates, they will want to talk to you, too.

Here is a sample letter:

SUBJECT LINE: Reference the job position and include your name for this subject line

Dear Kevon,

Given that you are always seeking referrals with solid talent for your clients, I am reaching out to introduce myself as a potential source of referrals for you, and as a potential candidate for consideration.

As a rising CFO / finance executive, I have done ___, ___, ___, and ___. My experience shows I have successfully turned around financially challenged organizations with redundant profit streams and led them to a more secure future. If you have clients in the ___ arena that could benefit from this background, it could be beneficial for us to chat.

If you'd like to, let me know convenient times for you to have a 15-20 minute chat, or here's a link to my schedule if this is more convenient. Looking forward to connecting when the time is right.

Sincerely,
Lorraine
Phone/email/LinkedIn URL

STAY-ON-THE-RADAR FOLLOW-UP COVER LETTER E-NOTE

This is my secret weapon. I am a huge fan of the "stay-on-the-radar" follow-up letter. Let me show you what one looks like and then explain the rationale behind it.

Here is a sample stay-on-the-radar e-note:

SUBJECT LINE: Following up on [REFERENCE POSITION YOU APPLIED FOR HERE]

Hi Maria,

I'm reaching out to simply stay on your radar and reiterate my interest in the ____ position we discussed on x/x/xx. I know we're awaiting feedback and things can often take longer than expected. No worries. I know you'll circle back when you know the next steps or if a different direction is being taken. I simply wanted to stay connected and share my continued enthusiasm.

No need to reply, as I know you will when you have an update. As I stated, simply staying on your radar.

Be well,

Lisa

Phone/email/LinkedIn URL

Why does the stay-on-the-radar e-note work?

I almost always get closure at some point when I send this e-note. It may not happen on the first send. And my record in sending this e-note is once every other week for 12 weeks before I got closure.

(Yeah, I don't give up.)

And in this case, I also received a positive response, so it doubly worked.

Here is why I believe it works.

- There is nothing left on the reader's to-do list — especially if there is no update to give.

There's no expectation for the reader to reply with an answer like, "Yeah, I don't have any information yet." Which is probably one of the recruiter's most hated to-do items. They have hundreds of candidates in limbo and they would make this call or write this email all day long if they had to reply to everyone. So if you reach out but DON'T put an expectation on the reader to do one more thing they don't have time to do, or want to do, this puts you in the "wow, this person gets it" pile. That can't hurt.

- Even if the reader doesn't reply, they probably read your e-note and noticed you.

How do I know? Think of your social media feeds — how many people do you know who reveal details of their lives to people they've never talked to, or haven't talked to in years, about their kids, vacation aspirations, family deaths, mental states, and what they ate for dinner last night? We feel like we've caught up with people even if we haven't seen them for ages. Well, I believe the same thing happens in emails. People read your e-note, mentally note that you're still interested, and feel caught up with you without an email exchange or a conversation.

- You free yourself from rejection and protect your mental health.

This may sound over-dramatic, but this is important. Think of it this way: if you send twenty follow-up e-notes ending in, "Let me know the status of my candidacy" and nineteen people don't reply... you may feel really crappy by the lack of replies, yes? But if you send twenty e-notes with the "I don't expect you to reply" vibe, there is no rejection to be felt. You've set yourself up to be happy when you get a reply and not sad when you don't. It's subtle, but huge in maintaining positive mental health during a job search.

- Recruiters and hiring managers lose a lot of control of the hiring process once it involves another person.

If you acknowledge this fact in your cover letter e-notes and follow-up e-notes, it shows you understand — and people want understanding more than ever. Cover letter e-notes and their correlating short, empathetic, follow-up e-notes work by showing that you're understanding and empathetic, while still going after your goals.

NEXT STEPS

Work through this book, taking the action steps throughout — and you'll have a much greater chance of landing that perfect job interview.

And when you've had the interview — do you follow up?

If not, it's time to work on your thank-you letters so you can refresh the interviewer's memory about what you can bring to the employer and how you can add value in this position.

Head over to jobthankyouletters.com and take the next step to landing your dream job.

ALSO BY LISA RANGEL

The Job Landing Mindset

The Six-Figure Resume

ABOUT THE AUTHOR

Lisa Rangel is the founder and managing director of Chameleon Resumes, named a Forbes Top 100 Career Website. She was a moderator of LinkedIn premium groups and career blogger for 8 years. As a recruitment professional since 1996 and as a Cornell University graduate, Lisa has held management and producer roles in numerous companies, ranging from international recruitment conglomerates to focused executive search firms.

In Chameleon Resumes, she has assembled the best team of resume writers and job search consultants who all have prior search firm and corporate recruiting experience—Chameleon is the only firm of its kind! Lisa and her team know first hand which resumes get a response. They've reviewed thousands of resumes over the years and helped top recruiters and talent for top organizations, working with clients in 88 countries.

Lisa is a member of the National Resume Writers' Association and Professional Association of Resume Writers and Career Coaches. She has been featured in person, online and in print on Fast Company, Forbes, LinkedIn, Newsweek, Money, Business Insider, CNBC, BBC, Crain's New York, Chicago Tribune, CIO Magazine, American Marketing Association, eFinancial Careers, The Vault, Monster, U.S. News & World Report, Good Morning America, Fox Business News and many other reputable publications.

She is the author of nine books, creator of the Get Hired Fast job-landing training series found at JobLandingAcademy.com, and a serial advice giver through her website ChameleonResumes.com. You can sign up to get advice from Lisa directly into your inbox from:

https://chameleonresumes.com/get-daily-career-tips/

 linkedin.com/in/lisarangel

www.ingramcontent.com/pod-product-compliance
Lightning Source LLC
Chambersburg PA
CBHW020548080526
44583CB00013B/1059